GW00707427

Prehistoric Marcham

The excavations at Marcham revealed a complex of prehistoric features da[...] to the late Iron Age. The discovery of thousands of pottery sherds and ani[...] Age suggests that people were eating and drinking here although this ma[...] rather than being normal domestic refuse.

While the site lacks clear evidence of domestic habitation, it does have some very unusual prehistoric features. To the east of the arena, an oval cluster of intercutting pits, apparently set inside a boundary of some kind, produced a particularly rich array of Iron Age finds. Some of these pits also contained human burials, reinforcing the idea that this area had some type of special status for the Iron Age people.

Moving to the area in and around the Roman temple and its sacred enclosure to the west, more unusual prehistoric features were found. What was the function of the huge barrel-shaped enclosure south of the Roman temple – perhaps some form of prehistoric ceremonies took place here?

Another strange ditched feature lay directly under the Roman 'rotunda' shrine inside the *temenos* area. The abnormally wide ditch was constructed to leave two 'islands' inside it and enclosed a small place in the centre where a timber building stood. Was something placed on these 'islands' to protect the sanctity of a shrine structure in the centre? Pits and post-holes inside this space contained votive items including a late Iron Age miniature sword and shield and a ploughshare, possibly related to a prehistoric fertility cult.

Evidence for prehistoric shrine sites in Britain is extremely rare, so the one at Marcham makes the early story of the site as remarkable as the Roman one.

Iron Age ring-headed pin

◄ ◄ ◄ Fold out to see the whole timeline

Iron Age / Mid Iron Age 700 BC - 100 BC	Late Iron Age / Early Roman 100 BC - AD 100	Mid Roman AD 100 - 275	Late Roman AD 275 - 410	Early Saxon AD 425 - 650

The Main Sacred Structures in the Roman Period

In the Roman period the site became a thriving temple complex. Key features of this complex were the large circular arena in the north-west and the square temple building and circular 'rotunda' shrine inside the walled sacred enclosure or *temenos* to the east. The buildings within the *temenos* would have been a major focus of worship on the site but other small shrine structures and a ritual shaft have been found between the *temenos* and the arena. It was common for a number of different deities to be worshipped at large temple complexes like Marcham.

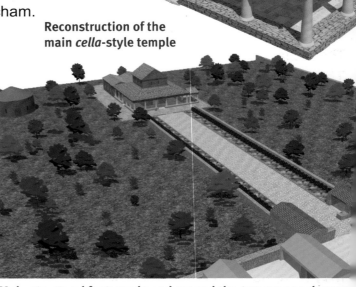

Reconstruction of the main *cella*-style temple

The Sacred Enclosure

The main temple building here was of a classical square *cella* form surrounded by an open walkway. Our own excavations and those in the 20th century established that it was built around AD 80-90, with a three room annexe being added at a later date. Painted plaster and hundreds of cut-down squares of red tile called *tesserae* have been found in the vicinity of this building, indicating the interior had decorated plaster walls and tessellated floors.

Visitors would pass statues on either side of the *temenos* entrance as they walked down the gravel path leading to the main temple.

Main structural features in and around the *temenos* enclosure

Excavations of the temple path found many Roman coins, some dating to as late as the early 5th century, probably representing votive offerings. Inside the enclosure animals would be sacrificed to the gods, as witnessed by the discovery of a sheep burial with a small libation pot inside the *temenos* wall. Small stone altars, donated by wealthy visitors, would have dotted the area inside the *temenos* walls.

The *cella* would have housed a large cult statue although which deity this was remains a mystery. Fragments of two pottery figures found here might be significant. The first was the broken head of a small red-painted bull figurine and the second a large ceramic animal horn, probably derived from a much larger bull figurine. Before the Roman period, bulls were sacred beasts to Iron Age people, symbolising strength, and this worship continued into the Roman period through the eastern Roman cult of Mithras, the soldiers' god, which was also associated with bulls.

Sheep burial with libation pot

The Arena

The arena was defined by a low circular bank and an inner stone wall plastered and painted to look like ashlar blocks. Pedestals for either statues or a stage and a mysterious stone building were found at the northern and southern points of the arena circuit respectively. Worshippers probably stood on the banks to watch religious plays and ceremonies, an essential part of Roman religious practice. The presence of water may have been an important reason for the siting of this temple complex, as the centre of the arena was habitually wet from rising ground water in rainy

seasons. A long stone drain was built to keep the arena dry, and perhaps to keep the 'sacred' water pure. The drain outflowed into a boggy area near the river Ock and the large number of Roman finds in this area, such as coins and fine quality tablewares, is suggestive of votive offerings and feasting.

Gods and Offerings

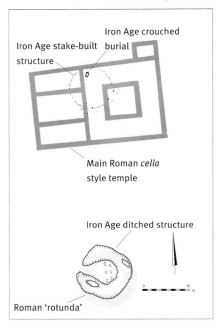

Iron Age crouched burial

Iron Age stake-built structure

Main Roman *cella* style temple

Iron Age ditched structure

Roman 'rotunda'

The Marcham site was a place for worship long before the Romans came to Britain. Lying directly underneath the *cella* and 'rotunda' Roman temples were two Iron Age structures whose function was probably ritual rather than domestic. Other parts of the temple complex, like the Roman shrine over a coin-filled shaft between two prehistoric pits, also show there was a long history of religious practices in this sacred space. Even after the Roman temple site was abandoned, early Saxon settlers buried their dead in a cemetery nearby and one important Saxon male was buried close to the main temple itself.

In the prehistoric period items of food, drink, tools, and animal sacrifices would have been offered to deities of natural places and things; high status offerings such as full-sized and model weapons and tools are also found in rivers, pools and pits. At our site, the miniature sword and shield found under the 'rotunda' are similar examples.

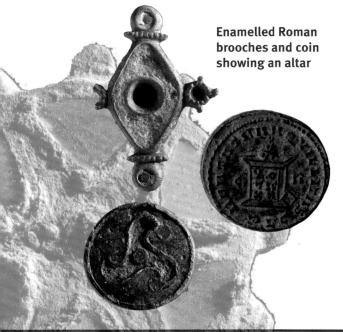

Enamelled Roman brooches and coin showing an altar

Rare repoussé *Ad Locutio* Roman brooch

The image of two Celtic-style horsemen facing Roman troops, with an imperial eagle below, was based on a Hadrianic coin showing the Emperor Hadrian addressing his troops. The replacement of the Emperor with native horsemen is an example of a Romano-British hybrid. The repoussé construction technique is more native Iron Age than Roman, as are the horsemen, but the main design is strongly Roman.

During the Roman period the range and number of offerings increases hugely, as does the choice of deities. The rich might offer stone altars or an animal sacrifice, while the poor might only offer food or scraps of metal. At Marcham the most common Roman offerings are coins, jewellery, small tools for cosmetic or medical use, and metal sheet or fittings.

Which gods were worshipped at the site? Probably more than one which were a mix of Roman and 'Romanised' Iron Age deities. We found no inscriptions to reveal their names, but some votive offerings supply clues. Mercury is the Roman god of travel and commerce, so the discovery of thousands of coins and some shoe shaped brooches may be offerings to that god.

Intaglio or seal-stone showing the goddess Ceres holding a sheaf of wheat

Fragments of Roman scale armour and an Achilles warrior intaglio may be linked to Mars, the god of war. Bracelets and medical tools may be female offerings to Bona Dea or Juno for help with fertility and childbirth, and the beautiful intaglio featuring Ceres, the goddess of agriculture, may suggest she too was worshipped here.

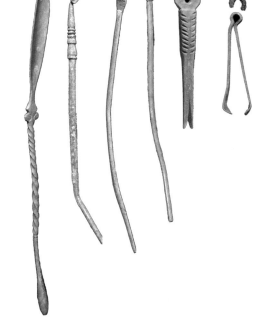

Selection of Roman medical/cosmetic tools from the site

Fragment of Roman scale armour

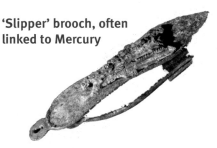

'Slipper' brooch, often linked to Mercury

Water and Ritual – the Roman Waterlogged Pit

This deep waterlogged pit situated by the River Ock is well below the water table, creating the anaerobic conditions which preserve rare organic objects such as wood and leather normally lost to archaeology. It had 'steps' cut down into it and was next to an area of decorative stone cobbling surrounded by box hedging within a formal garden area, suggesting the pit had some special status beyond that of an ordinary rubbish pit.

The finds in this pit also suggest it wasn't for discarded rubbish. They included a hobnailed Roman shoe or boot; two complete Roman storage jars, both cleanly and intentionally perforated with something like a spear; a small cut-down writing tablet; a finely-made, drum-shaped willow basket with its base cleanly cut off; and part of a cattle skull with the muzzle and horns deliberately removed.

The leather Roman shoe with hobnails

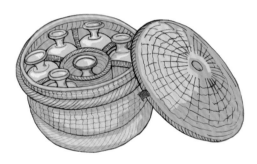

Reconstruction of a medical basket similar in form to the Marcham basket

These objects were placed in the pit in the late Roman period, sometime in the 4th century and before the temple site went out of use in the early 5th century. Such ritual offerings were not the act of a Christian community and this either signifies continuing pagan worship at the site, after AD 313 when Constantine made Christianity the official Roman religion, or perhaps an 'ending' ceremony to herald adoption of the new Christian faith.

The water-logged pit during excavation

Trench plan showing the waterlogged pit and associated features

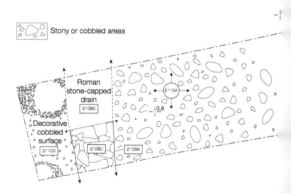

Stony or cobbled areas

Roman stone-capped drain
21060

Decorative cobbled surface

21103   21060   21059

21104

0.8

Interestingly, all of these objects were either very worn or were ritually 'killed' or defaced before deposition. This makes them unfit for use in the world of the living, so they are marked as offerings to the gods or the spirits. There are many examples across prehistoric and Roman Britain of ritually 'killed' objects left as offerings in sacred watery places like our pit at Marcham and perhaps the arena and the place where its drain ends. Watery places such as lakes, rivers, and wells were seen as portals to the shadowy under-world of the gods and the spirits – literally 'gateways to the gods'.

The wooden writing tablet

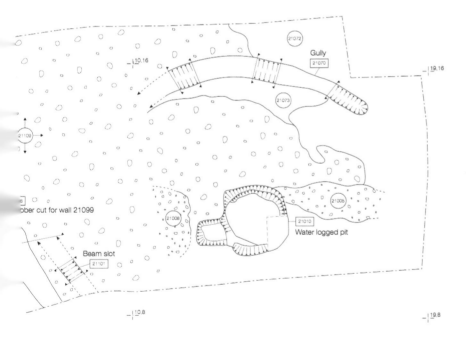

One of the two 'stabbed' grey ware jars

Belief in an Afterlife?

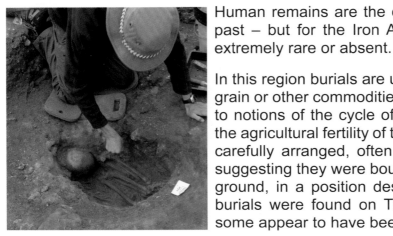

Iron Age crouched burial

Human remains are the closest link we have to the people in the past – but for the Iron Age in most areas of Britain, graves are extremely rare or absent.

In this region burials are usually found in pits dug for the storage of grain or other commodities, the choice of receptacle possibly linked to notions of the cycle of life, death and rebirth as symbolized by the agricultural fertility of the grain. The bodies appear to have been carefully arranged, often very tightly bent at the hips and knees suggesting they were bound or wrapped before being placed in the ground, in a position described as crouched. A number of these burials were found on Trendles Field and nearby and unusually some appear to have been placed in specially dug graves.

The first discovery came during an earlier excavation at the Noah's Ark Inn in 1964 when a skeleton of an adolescent was found within the circular stake-built structure, which was later to be overlain by a Romano-British shrine. In 2008 we found that burial was mirrored further to the east by one of similar age, arranged in the same tightly contracted way.

Further east, a more formal area of burial was discovered with at least seven shallow graves. Unusually one of the burials was found with grave goods - a bronze ring close to its throat. The graves were interspersed with pits containing animal bones, more complete than was usual from the remains of meals, with some pits containing parts of birds and horses, or the skulls of dogs and cattle, suggesting these were specially placed deposits or offerings.

Roman Burials

Over 300 cremations and inhumations were discovered at the late Roman and Anglo-Saxon cemetery across the road so the discovery of eight skeletons in the arena bank was unexpected. The bodies lacked grave goods and all lay on an east-west alignment, which suggests they were Christian. One was found with its hand around its throat. Examination has shown that in life this person was at least partially deaf which might have affected speech. Was the hand, placed in such a way, indicating this?

Radiocarbon dating has shown these people were contemporary with those buried in the cemetery across the road, but why they were buried here is uncertain. A minor genetic condition found in a number of the skeletons might indicate that this was a family group or at least members of a small close-knit community.

Sea urchins

Reports exist from around the world of fossil sea urchins being found in Neolithic and later graves. They were first noticed here in 1920 by Dudley Buxton when excavating at the cemetery. He noted that they appeared to have been placed opposite the joints of some of the skeletons. Twenty-six were found when excavating the Iron Age area on Trendles Field. Most were heart urchins and they might have been deliberately chosen for their shape.

Their presence only in this part of the site and their association with specially placed animal remains in pits and graves suggests they had a special meaning to the people buried here. One had been sawn and perforated and might have been worn as a talisman.

Romano-British extended burial

The Pottery Assemblage

The temple site at Marcham produced tens of thousands of fragments of prehistoric and Roman pottery. These vessels may have been used in religious feasts and celebrations, as well as by visitors to the various shrines who needed food and

drink. As part of our Heritage Lottery funded community project, the Trendles Project volunteers have identified the main fabric and vessel form types in the pottery assemblage and recorded the incidence of different types across the site. Their work has highlighted many interesting facts about this assemblage.

Equipment used in drawing pots

Prehistoric fine and coarse wares

A few rare Neolithic decorated sherds and the remains of a large Bronze Age bucket found at the site testify to some very early prehistoric activity in this field, probably from the 3rd and 2nd millennia BC. However most of the prehistoric pottery is of Iron Age date, deriving from a network of pits and ditches across the site. As well as the usual large coarse ware cooking and storage vessels made of clay tempered with shell and quartz inclusions, we have also identified many smaller vessels, made with fine sandy clays and sometimes burnished and decorated with incised geometric

Rim from a hand-made Iron Age pot

designs. These finer vessels were often shaped into globular and elegant carinated bowls, some finished to a deep glossy red by the application of haematite powder. These were the eating and drinking vessels of the Iron Age community who worshipped and visited here.

Roman tablewares

In the Roman period the range of pottery shapes and fabric types increased hugely at Marcham, as on other Roman sites In Britain. This was due to the growth of a commercial pottery industry, initially on the continent, and then increasingly in Romanised Britain, with large regional kiln centres producing a huge range of table-wares to satisfy a developing consumer market.

The Roman pottery assemblage at Marcham includes many fine imported continental vessels such as bowls and beautifully decorated drinking beakers from Roman Gaul, the Rhineland and Italy. Also found were large quantities of bowls, mortaria, flagons, and drinking vessels from the commercial Oxford pottery kilns. These were all the fashionable tablewares of the Roman world and testify to the wealth and status of the visitors to the temple site. Products from many other regional potteries, such as black-burnished dishes from the Dorset area, fine coloured drinking cups from the Nene Valley kilns near Northampton, and sturdy Savernake ware cooking jars from Wiltshire, show how widely connected the temple site and its visitors were with national markets.

Roman samian ware sherd with hunting scene

Roman kitchenwares

Simpler large storage jars and cooking pots were also found, usually made in a coarser fabric than the fine wares and tempered with inclusions like local fossil shell, quartz, and recycled crushed pottery called grog. Inclusions helped to spread the heat while these large pots were being fired, reducing the risk of them breaking in the kiln. Whilst the majority of the Roman fine wares were wheel-made, some of the coarser wares were still being hand-made, right through the Roman period. The wide range of Roman pottery types found at Marcham indicates that food and drink was prepared and consumed here in large quantities from the 1st century to the end of the 4th century AD.

Reconstructing a fine grey ware jar

Animal Remains

Animal bones are amongst the most common finds on archaeological sites. They can reveal a great deal about human activity and how people interacted with animals. Our main goals in studying them is to understand the processes of human exploitation - whether the animals were domesticated or hunted, raised for food, sacrificed, or venerated. Our findings are providing insights into diet, the economy of the site and the various activities being carried out there. Looking at how this pattern changes across the site and through time forms an important component of the Trendles story.

Volunteers laying out a sheep burial from the temple

Domesticated animals were much smaller than they are today and by studying their remains we can begin to understand the development of livestock farming and economy. Volunteers working on the Trendles Project have learnt to identify animal bones by species and where possible their approximate age and gender.

Identifying butchery marks on the bones where the animals were cut into joints of meat, and filleting marks where meat was taken off the bone is helping us to understand how the carcasses were processed and something about how animal products were being used. The pattern of gnaw marks left on bones after they were discarded by people gives us clues to other species of animal that were present on the site.

As would be expected from an important Iron Age and Romano-British religious site, animal sacrifices and special offerings of parts of animals have been found, with a particular concentration around the Roman temple and shrines, and the Iron Age burial ground in the east. However, the majority of the animal bone from Trendles Field comprises thousands of fragments of bones and teeth, much of which is the discarded remains from butchery or meals. They are from the same domesticated species we see today, sheep, cattle and pig, with people enjoying a varied diet

Cow skeleton ('Daisy') found in the arena bank

with good quality cuts of meat. Horses and dogs were also present on the site, along with chickens, thought to have been introduced in the late Iron Age, and possibly pheasant, a bird brought over by the Romans. There is little evidence for the hunting of wild animals. Oysters were harvested and consumed in large quantities in the Roman period, the discarded shells found amongst the Roman features on the site.

Bone counters found at Marcham

Most of the food animals were slaughtered as soon as they had reached a good size but animals that were used for traction such as horses and oxen were kept for as long as possible. It would have taken time to train the animals and from the wear on horse teeth we can see they were often kept for much longer than the main food animals.

Craft Working

Bone is harder than wood but more easily worked and would have been readily accessible. It also survives well in the ground in this area. Large numbers of bone objects were found during the excavations including weaving tools, needles, hairpins and gaming counters. Sawn offcuts of bone, antler and horn were also found providing evidence that these or similar objects were being made on the site.

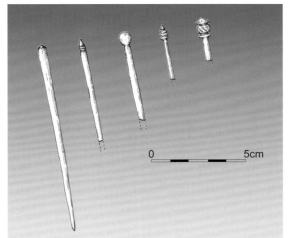

0   5cm

An extraordinary number of bone pins deposited in two adjacent areas of small upright stones is indicative of a special ritual, to whom or what is unclear; but possibly a female deity. A sightline from the temple complex to the shrines where the pins were found may suggest a form of 'processional' way between the temple and the arena.

The Trendles Project and the Community – Outreach

One of the main objectives of the Project was to involve as many local people as possible, with outreach playing an important part for those who retained an interest in our activities but were unable to give their time on a regular basis as a Trendles Project Volunteer. Over the course of the 3-year project a range of events were organized to appeal to a wide cross-section of the local community.

Open days, held at the excavation site at Manor Farm, offered guided tours of the former trenches and a chance to catch up on our recent findings. Iron Age re-enactment and story-telling, and craft activities such as weaving, pottery-making and basketry allowed families to step back in time and engage in some living history. Our Roman food stall was always a popular venue.

Marcham Primary School visit

We were especially delighted to welcome pupils from Marcham Primary School who joined us at a special open day where they learned about the project and took part in activities including test-pitting and surveying, in which the children participated with gusto.

Finds identification days proved popular throughout the course of the project, as were our mini-exhibitions at local schools and libraries. Talks requested by local history and archaeology societies, U3A groups and the local scout troop were always enjoyable, and our volunteers did a wonderful job of passing on their knowledge.

A four month exhibition at Abingdon Museum in 2015 included a series of workshops for local schools. Our Education Officer and volunteers guided the children around the exhibits and provided

Open days invited visitors to get 'hands on' with the pr

hands-on experience in recording some of the objects that had been excavated. Themed family drop-in sessions at the museum were also provided throughout the school summer holidays. The available activities were linked not only to the exhibition but to the different areas of work carried out by members of the project, and it was rewarding to see so many children learning about archaeology in such an enthusiastic manner.

Finds Identification Days

Last, but not least, have been the visits to local primary schools, many taking place in conjunction with specially arranged Roman-themed school days where our box of Roman finds from the excavation was particularly popular.

Learning about finds from a Trendles Project volunteer

Volunteers ran a Roman food stall at Cirencester museum

...g archaeological techniques

It has been a pleasure to pass on our love of archaeology to future generations, and to teach them about their rich past in a local context.

Trendles Volunteer Project

Many people in Britain have the opportunity to take part in archaeological excavations but few are able to follow the full archaeological process from excavation to finds processing, stratigraphic work and then analysis. The Trendles Project is one of the few that allows local people to do just that.

Identifying and recording animal bone

Thanks to a 3-year grant from the Heritage Lottery Fund, local people have worked alongside trained archaeologists making an active contribution to a major archaeological publication. Hundreds of thousands of fragments of pottery and animal bone from eleven seasons of excavation have been identified and catalogued. Our volunteers also undertook the work of checking and synthesising thousands of site records and drawings dealing with stratigraphic relationships. This has resulted in a searchable database with key information on all the archaeological contexts dug on the site.

Working on the site records

Site plan and trench records

Local history walk with one of our volunteers

We welcomed visitors and helpers from all areas of the community